Introduction

Iran's intransigence over its nuclear development program is only the latest episode in which Tehran has made international news headlines and is at least part of the reason 27 percent of Americans consider Iran as Washington's "greatest menace."[1] Iran's February 2006 announcement it would resume enriching uranium underscored the tension that has existed between Washington and Tehran since the 1979 Iranian Revolution. Then, after insurrectionists seized the U.S. Embassy in Tehran and held Americans hostage for 444-days, Washington cut formal relations and has since relied on other countries such as France and Russia to deal with Tehran.[2] But it may be time for Washington to begin dealing directly with Tehran rather than working through proxies.

After all, Iran is both regionally and strategically significant. "Its population is estimated to be nearly 70 million, and it sits astride the intersection of Central, Southwest, and South Asia, as well as the Persian Gulf. In addition to these geographical and human resources, Iran is also endowed with the world's second-largest gas reserve (it has 15 percent of the total world gas reserves) and the third-largest reserve of oil (9 percent of the global oil reserve)."[3] Yet Iran is disconnected from the world's "Functioning Core" of countries, thus far having eluded integration or globalization.[4] It therefore requires careful attention from analysts, U.S. military planners, and policymakers, especially in light of its important ongoing demographic changes.

This paper considers one of Iran's most important demographic challenges – its youth bulge – and its potential impacts on U.S. national security. The paper begins by summarizing the

---

[1] Zogby Polling, 14 Feb 06. Available on-line at http://www.zogby.com.
[2] C. Christine Fair. "Iran: What Future for the Islamic State?" Chapter Four of *The Muslim World after 9/11*, a RAND Corporation Project Air Force study dated 2004, p. 207.
[3] Ibid, p. 207.
[4] Thomas P.M. Barnett, *The Military's New Map: War and Peace in the Twenty-First Century*. G.P. Putnam's Sons, New York, 2004.

broad academic literature and existing schools of thought regarding the relationships between youth bulges in general and political instability. It then uses two models from the U.S.-government sponsored Political Instability Task Force to analyze Iran's situation, comparing circumstances prior the 1979 Islamic Revolution to circumstances today. The paper concludes by examining U.S. national security implications and by recommending potential courses of action for policymakers, planners, and Iran analysts.

Context

Among the myriad long-term issues Washington must consider, Iran is once again experiencing a youth bulge similar to the one it experienced in the late 1970s. It is just one of many countries in the region and in the world facing such a youth bulge, which can generically be defined as "extraordinary large youth cohorts relative to the adult population."[5] For example, over half the populations of Egypt, Syria, Saudi Arabia, and Iraq are under 25 years old, while over 60 percent of Pakistan's and Afghanistan's populations are under 25 years old. These youth bulges have been spawned by large increases in fertility rates and large decreases in infant mortality rates (IMR) over the past 50 years.[6] After Iran's 1979 revolution, the government sponsored a fertility drive that pushed Iran's official total fertility rate (TFR) well beyond the replacement-level TFRs of most industrialized nations, leading to today's youth bulge.[7]

---

[5] Henrik Urdal, "The Devil in the Demographics: The Effect of Youth Bulges on Domestic Armed Conflict, 1950 - 2000." The World Bank, Social Development Papers, Conflict Prevention & Reconstruction, Paper No. 14, July 2004, p. 1.

[6] Nader Kabbani and Ekta Kothari, *Youth Employment in the MENA Region: A Situational Assessment*. The World Bank. Social Protection Discussion Paper No. 0534, September 2005, p. 12. Besides fertility rates and IMR, other factors that affect the size, shape and duration of youth bulges include changes in human longevity, the impact of HIV on the populace, and emigration.

[7] During this fertility drive, Iran's Supreme Leader Ayatollah Ruhollah Khomeini exhorted Iranian mothers to breed, telling them "My soldiers are still infants." Elaine Sciolino, "Radicalism: Is the Devil in the Demographics?", New York Times, 9 December 2001. Also, according to Mohammad Jalal Abbasi-Shavazi a professor in the Department of Demography, Faculty of Social Sciences, University of Tehran, Iran's total fertility rate (TFR is defined as the average number of children born to a woman during her lifetime) has changed dramatically since the early 1970s. It began increasing in the late stages of the Shah's regime (1976 onward), accelerated after the 1979 Islamic Revolution, and peaked around 1984 at about 6.5. Iran's TFR subsequently subsided, dropping precipitously after

The figures below illustrate how developing countries' population age pyramids differ from those of industrialized nations, which generally have lower fertility rates and IMRs than developing nations, and how Iran's 2005 profile shows a youth bulge. Note that at left the shape is actually pyramidal, meaning there has as yet been no decrease in the youthful population (no decrease in fertility rates), while Iran's demographic "pyramid" shows a pronounced "bulge."

Photo Removed Due to Copyright Restrictions

Fig. 1, Population Age Pyramids

The bulge shape is partly because the country's birth rate plummeted after Iran's "ruling clerics concluded in the late 1980s that the population increase was disastrous for the economy and launched a massive family planning program."[10] Despite its robust and effective family planning programs, however, there remains in Iran today a youth surfeit that will cause its

---

1990 to 2.69 in 1996. See his "Below replacement-level fertility in Iran: Progress and Prospects," a paper prepared for the IUSSP Seminar on International Perspectives on Low Fertility: Trends, Theories and Policies, Tokyo, March 21-23, 2001, p. 2-3 and p. 9. See also the Population Reference Bureau's (PRB) 2005 World Population Data Sheet, which estimates the worldwide mean TFR at 2.7. According to the PRB, "More Developed" countries have a mean TFR of 1.6, "Less Developed" countries have a mean TFR of 3.0, and "Less Developed countries excluding China" have a mean of 3.5. To compare, the United States' TFR was an estimated 2.0, Europe's mean was 1.4, and Iran's was estimated by PRB at 2.1 in 2005. Found at http://www.prb.org/.

[8] Brian Nichiporuk. "The Security Dynamics of Demographic Factors." A RAND Monograph Report, 2000, p. 14.

[9] Source: U.S. Census Bureau, International Database, found at http://www.census.gov/ipc/www/idbnew.html. Iran population pyramids for 1976, 1986 and 1996, and 1986-2015 are attached at the end of this paper at Table 4.

[10] Sciolino, 9 December 2001.

population's absolute size to continue to grow for the next 20-25 years.[11] If Iran is able to

capitalize on it, such a youth bulge could provide the country with a "demographic dividend."[12]

According to Herbert Moller, one of the first academics to seriously consider the impact

of youth bulges on political stability, in any country "The presence of a large contingent of

young people in a population may make for a cumulative process of innovation and social

growth; it may lead to elemental, directionless action-out behavior; it may destroy old

institutions and elevate new elites to power; and the unemployed energies of the young may be

organized and directed by totalitarian rulers."[13] Youth bulges may therefore provide an impetus

for progress or instead intensify or exacerbate existing problems. For example, youth bulges

may strain a country's leadership abilities and agendas, environment (especially its natural

resources) or its social infrastructure (especially its labor market and health care and educational

systems) beyond the point of failure, thus leading to political instability and increasing the risk of

violent conflict.[14]

---

[11] According to Kabbani, as a result of its family planning program, Iran's fertility rates fell by 70 percent between 1989 and 2002. See Kabbani, p. 11-12.

[12] According to Ellen Laipson, Iran would have to implement appropriate economic and social policies to effectively harness the energies of its growing work force to increase its economic growth and improve standards of living. See Ellen Laipson, "The Middle East's Demographic Transition: What Does it Mean?" *Journal of International Affairs*, Fall 2002, vol. 56, no. 1, p. 176.

[13] Herbert Moller, "Youth as a Force in the Modern World," *Comparative Studies in Society and History*, Vol. 10, No. 3 (April, 1968), p. 260.

[14] See Graham Fuller, "The Youth Factor: The New Demographics of the Middle East and the Implications for U.S. Policy." DRAFT, 18 January 2003, p. 6; Nichiporuk, 2000, p. 23; Urdal, 2004, p. 1; John. L. Helgerson, "The National Security Implications of Global Demographic Change." Address to the Denver World Affairs Council and the Better World Campaign, Denver, CO, 30 April 2002. Found at http://www.au.af.mil/au/awc/awcgate/cia/helgerson2.htm; and the Central Intelligence Agency's (CIA) *Long-Term Demographic Trends*, 2001. Found at http://www.cia.gov/cia/reports/Demo_Trends_For_Web.pdf. Colin Kahl, in his article, "Demographic Change, Natural Resources and Violence: The Current Debate," in the *Journal of International Affairs*, Fall 2002, vol. 56, no. 1, lists more strains of youth bulges: pressure for government-sponsored development projects; demands for employment, housing, schools, sanitation, energy, and lower prices; increased fiscal strains; erosion of the state's administrative capacity; and ultimately erosion of the state's legitimacy.

History & Literature Review

This is not to say that youth bulges are the sole cause of political instability, let alone conflict. In fact, few if any academics would argue youth bulges are necessary or sufficient to cause political instability by themselves. Instead, most agree there are complex biological, psychological, demographic, economic, and political interactions that cause instability and conflict.[15] In their 1999 article "Male Age Composition and Severity of Conflicts," Christian Mesquida and Neil Wiener tested whether countries' ethnic compositions and levels of fractionalization, population sizes, population densities, and levels of urbanization played roles in explaining the onset of political instability.[16] Their empirical tests generally matched others', controlling for each of these factors but finding no one factor plays a singularly causal role.[17] Instead, the tests only generally agree youth bulges play at least some role in increasing the risk of political instability; their exact level of impact is debatable. The academic literature surrounding the debate can be summarized within four major rationales: the "Fact of a Youth Bulge," "Generational Consciousness," "Ignition Source," and "Regime Type" arguments.

Before considering these rationales, however, it is worth considering the two major schools of thought on how best to operationalize the concept of a youth bulge. The first,

---

[15] Christian Mesquida and Neil Wiener use the term *polemology* for the study of causes of wars, which they regard as "…regularly occurring natural phenomena that have explanations in the realms of biology, psychology, demography, economics, and political science." Christian G Mesquida and Neil I. Wiener. "Male Age Composition and Severity of Conflicts." *Politics and the Life Sciences*, September 1999, 18, p. 187.

[16] Ibid, p. 181-187. Mesquida and Wiener also mused that a country's physical characteristics – such as whether it is divided by mountains, forests or rivers; its amount of arable land; and its amount and type of mineral resources – may help explain the onset of political instability. For example, does a more urbanized populace mean youth will have contact with a "vastly greater variety of personalities, situations and experiences that sharply and differentially affect the development process," thus leading to greater likelihood of political instability? See Graham Fuller, 2003, p. 12. And what impact do a country's size and level of urbanization have? How, when and why can a primarily urban popular mobilization sufficiently affect the entire country to overthrow a government, as in Iran in 1979? See Jack Goldstone, "Toward A Fourth Generation Of Revolutionary Theory." *Annual Review of Political Science*, 2001, 4: p. 143.

[17] Mesquida and Wiener, 1999, p. 187; Nichiporuk, 2000, p. 39; Jack A. Goldstone, Ted Robert Gurr, Barbara Harff, Marc A. Levy, Monty G. Marshall, Robert H. Bates, David L. Epstein, Colin H. Kahl, Pamela T. Surko, John Ulfelder, and Alan N. Unger. *State Failure Task Force Report: Phase III Findings.* McLean, VA: Science Applications International Corporation (SAIC), 2000.

suggested by theorists such as Collier, Goldstone and Huntington, measures the size of youth

cohorts (people aged 15 to 24 years old) relative to the *total* population. The second, used by

Urdal and others, measures youth cohorts as 15-24 year-olds relative to the total *adult*

population, which is considered the populace aged 15 years and older. The difference in

definitions helps explain why the first school sees little link between bulges and the risk of

political instability, let alone infers a causal relationship, while the second school sees clear

linkages between youth bulges and instability and infers at least a small amount of causality.[18]

"Fact of" a Youth Bulge

The argument that youth bulges increase the risk of instability if not help cause political

instability is not new.[19] Youth bulges have historically coincided with political instability in

England in 1640; France in 1789, 1830, 1848 and 1968; Germany in 1812, 1848 and the 1930s

(the rise of Nazism);[20] Austria in 1848; China in 1960 and 1989; Indonesia in 1945 and 1965;

Hungary in 1956; Korea in 1960; the U.S. in the 1960s; and all over Eastern Europe in 1989-

1991.[21] In the wake of the Cold War's end, authors such as Robert Kaplan and Sam Huntington

argued demographic factors became more important than ever. Huntington's 1996 *Clash of*

Civilizations hypothesis actually depended on the existence of youth bulges, positing that youth

bulges beyond a certain, "critical level" – which he defined as occurring when the number of

young people aged 15-24 reached 20% of a country's total populace – made countries especially

---

[18] Henrik Urdal. "A Clash of Generations? Youth Bulges and Political Violence." Centre for the Study of Civil War, International Peace Research Institute, Oslo. Paper prepared for the Workshop on Conflict Research, January 2005, p.12.

[19] See Moller, 1968.

[20] Moller, 1968, p. 244. Moller posited Germany's large 1930s youth cohort began to enter the labor market during a major economic depression, helping lead to the rise of Nazism.

[21] See Urdal, 2004, 2, and Jack A. Goldstone, "Youth Bulges, Youth Cohorts, and their Contribution to Periods of Rebellion and Revolution," unpublished manuscript prepared for the John M. Olin Center for Strategic Studies, Harvard University, Center for International Affairs, 29 May 1999, p. 2.

prone to conflict.[22] After 9/11, some authors blamed youth bulges for both political instability in the Arab world and terrorist networks' effective international recruitment, especially when combined with a country's or a region's poor economic performance, limited economic development, and repressive social policies.[23]

At its core, the "Fact of a Youth Bulge" argument depends on little more than the existence of a youth bulge. Proponents argue that youth are more easily attracted to new ideas and are more likely to challenge authority, and that the sheer increase in the number of all youth increases the number of those likely to foment or participate in rebellious acts.[24] They argue "youth are not as psychologically or physically capable of understanding the consequences of their actions as adults," and are "generally not psychologically capable of weighing in realistic terms all the possible consequences of their actions."[25] They also argue that "…it is primarily the skewing of the national age distribution in favor of younger citizens that often puts extreme pressure on the educational, health care, sanitation, and economic infrastructures of developing nations that is the most decisive factor creating domestic instability."[26]

Supporters of this rationale explain young people are different from their elders because they are "…simply free, to a unique degree, of constraints that tend to make activism too time consuming or risky for other groups to engage in. Often freed from the demands of family, marriage, and full-time employment…[youth] are uniquely available to express their political

---

[22] See Robert Kaplan, "The Coming Anarchy," *Atlantic Monthly*, February, 1994; Lieutenant General Patrick M Hughes, USA. "Global Threats and Challenges to the United States and Its Interests Abroad," Statement for the Senate Select Committee on Intelligence, 5 Feb 1997 and Statement for the Senate Armed Services Committee on Intelligence, 6 Feb 1997. Found at http://www.fas.org/irp/congress/1997_hr/s970205.htm; and Samuel Huntington, *The Clash Of Civilizations And The Remaking Of World Order*. New York: Simon & Schuster, 1996, p. 259-261. Huntington later accedes that "Shifts in the demographic balances and youth bulges of 20 percent or more account for many of the intercivilizational [sic] conflicts of the late twentieth century. They do not, however, explain all of them." See p. 261.
[23] See Urdal, 2004, p. 1; and Fareed Zakaria, "The Politics of Rage: Why Do They Hate Us?" *Newsweek*, 15 October 2001, p. 22.
[24] Goldstone, 2001, p. 95; and Urdal, 2005, p. 9.
[25] Fuller, 2003, p. 23.
[26] Nichiporuk, 2000, p. 39.

values through action."[27] Thus, to this school of thought, the existence of youth, free from its

parents' obligations, explains political instability. But if the "Fact of a Youth Bulge" was

singularly causal, history would no doubt have seen much more political instability than it has.

Generational Consciousness

Since the "Fact of a Youth Bulge" argument fails to fully explain the relationship

between youth bulges and political instability, some academics have hypothesized that at some

point youth cohorts reach a point of self-consciousness in opposition to their elders where they

achieve "…awareness of belonging to a generation of extraordinary size and strength, enabling

them to act collectively."[28] Because this school of thought pits youth against older generations,

it uses the youth bulge definition comparing youth cohorts to the adult population vice the total

population. Within this rationale, one sub-element insists there must be a unifying experience

among the youth to establish their own identity group that is distinct from their parents, while the

opposing sub-element counters that a "…marked change in the size of a youth cohort, compared

to earlier ones, can itself form a kind of watershed experience that creates a distinctive world-

view on the part of that cohort."[29]

Either way, according to this rationale there is a seminal event or a major social change

that distinguishes the youth generation from preceding generations, leading to increased risk of

political instability. In Henrik Urdal's testing based on the operationalized definition of youth

bulges as youth cohorts compared to the adult populace, he finds:

---

[27] Doug McAdam, *Freedom Summer*. Oxford: Oxford University Press, 1988, p. 44.

[28] See Urdal, 2005, p. 3.

[29] See Karl Mannheim, "What is a Social Generation?" In *The Youth Revolution: The Conflict of Generations in Modern History*, edited by Anthony Esler, pp. 7-14. Lexington, MA: D.C. Heath, 1974; and Karl Mannheim, *From Karl Mannheim*. Edited by Kurt Wolff. 2nd ed. New Brunswick, NJ: Transaction Publishers, 1993, for more on this argument. The core of Mannheim's thought is that "…a youthful age-cohort can become a self-conscious generation in opposition to its elders only if it undergoes some unifying experience distinctive from that of their [sic] parents." Jack Goldstone cites examples from the post-World War Two era, writing that, "It was just such a post-war cohort, not only in the United States, but also in Western Europe, in Latin America, in China, in South Korea, and in Africa, that helped produce the global waves of idealistic rebellion in the 1960s." See Goldstone, 1999, p. 6.

The results clearly support the main hypothesis that large youth bulges increase the risk of armed conflict. An increase in youth bulges of one percentage point is associated with an increased likelihood of conflict of around 5 percent, and countries experiencing youth bulges of 35% run almost three times the risk of armed conflict compared to countries with an age structure equal to the year 2000 median for developed countries, all other variables at mean.[30]

There are major critiques of the "Generational Consciousness" argument, however, including its lack of attention to motives and opportunities for youth rebellion. Some also argue the possibility that the size of the youth cohort is more important than having a common experience in explaining the resulting political instability: "If it shares a distinctive, radicalizing experience, even a small youth cohort can adopt a rebellious stance."[31] Finally, like the "Fact of a Youth Bulge" argument, critics submit that the "Generational Consciousness" argument fails to adequately explain why, if large youth cohorts with distinct generational values are enough to always produce conflict, we have not seen more violent youth-led revolts.[32]

Ignition Source

Perhaps the Generational Consciousness argument fails to completely satisfy because youth bulges are neither necessary nor sufficient in and of themselves to fully explain political instability. Thus, the third major rationale argues that, while a youth bulge may provide fuel for the fire, there must first be a source for political instability to ignite. The "Ignition Source" may be either a better opportunity or a grievance. Mesquida and Wiener, for example, insist young males go to war primarily over the opportunity to obtain material resources, such as oil, water, or land.[33] They argue that "Men with few material assets may be more inclined to undertake risk in

---

[30] Urdal, 2005, p. 19. His results are attached at Table 3 at the back of this paper.
[31] Goldstone, 1999, p. 8.
[32] Urdal, 2004, p. 2.
[33] Mesquida and Wiener, 1999, p. 182. Robert Kaplan's February 1994 *Atlantic Monthly* article, "The Coming Anarchy," prophesied that, "To understand the events of the next fifty years, then, one must understand environmental scarcity, cultural and racial clash, geographic destiny, and the transformation of war." (p. 54) Kaplan called the environment – including the Earth's surging population and urban overcrowding – the national security issue of the twenty-first century, and pointed to Thomas Fraser Homer-Dixon's fall 1991 article "On the Threshold:

order to increase their access to resources, and competition can be driven to lethal levels," and that young people "...have more to gain and less to lose as a consequence of collective violence than do their elders."[34] While this argument dovetails nicely with the "Fact of a Youth Bulge" argument, it does little to explain why there have not been more youth-led revolts. If young people with fewer material resources than their predecessors always initiated conflict to eliminate those differences or create differences in their own favor, we would expect to have seen more such conflicts.

The grievance that arguably best explains when youth bulges help cause political instability is unemployment. Since youths are historically more likely to be unemployed than older generations, youth bulges exacerbate the problem because they increase the supply of labor unnaturally and substantially when they enter the labor market.[35] In Iran, for example, the World Bank estimates the share of youth among the unemployed at near 60% despite being only approximately 25% of the labor force (see Fig. 2 below).

Photo Removed Due to Copyright Restrictions

Fig. 2, Share of Youth Among the Unemployed & Among the Labor Force[36]

Environmental Changes as Causes of Acute Conflict" in the journal *International Security* as the seminal analysis of post-Cold War foreign policy. Kaplan writes, "In Homer-Dixon's view, future wars and civil violence will often arise from scarcities of resources such as water, cropland, forests, and fish." (Kaplan, 1994, p. 59) See also Nils Petter Gleditsch and Henrik Urdal, "Ecoviolence? Links Between Population Growth, Environmental Scarcity and Violent Conflict in Thomas Homer-Dixon's Work," in the *Journal of International Affairs*, Fall 2002, vol. 56, no. 1, pp. 283-302.
[34] Mesquida and Wiener, 1999, p. 182-183.
[35] Urdal, 2004, p. 2.
[36] Kabbani, 2005, p. 6. Note the rest of the region shares similar if not worse youth unemployment problems.

Thus, "…most theoretical works concerned with youth bulges point to limited absorption capacity of the labor market as the most important factor for causing grievances among youth."[37] The logic behind this assertion is that each youth bulge, by definition, includes a large pool of new labor. As this new labor pool looks for its first jobs – no doubt with high expectations – if the labor market cannot sufficiently absorb it, the result will be a large number of frustrated, unemployed young people.[38] For example, The World Bank estimates that Middle East and North African (MENA) countries must create 37 million new jobs over the next ten years to meet demands from first-time job seekers, plus an additional 19 million jobs to eliminate regional unemployment. These astounding numbers mean the number of current jobs would have to expand by an impossible two-thirds over the decade.[39]

The good news is that labor markets may effectively absorb these new entrants without completely eliminating unemployment if they are sufficiently flexible and efficient.[40] The bad news is that it is not clear what specific features make a labor market "sufficiently flexible and efficient" to ensure new cohorts are absorbed.[41] And when youth bulges coincide with periods of serious economic decline, according to the "Ignition Source" argument, they subsequently generate "despair among young people that moves them towards the use of violence."[42]

But unemployment is not homogeneous, and mere unemployment percent levels belie the concept's complexity. It has a gender component (more women are generally unemployed or

---

[37] Urdal, 2004, p. 3.

[38] The counter-argument, expressed by the World Bank's Kabbani, is "Empirical evidence suggests that macroeconomic conditions are more important determinants of both youth and adult unemployment rates than demographic changes." Kabbani, 2005, p. 15.

[39] Data from Laipson, 2002, p. 179.

[40] Kabbani argues that "…even though large numbers of jobs must be created to accommodate the young workers currently entering the labor force, *if* suitable jobs for these young workers are found, labor supply pressures are likely to ease in the near future." Kabbani, 2005, p. 14. Italics in the original.

[41] Ibid, p. 16.

[42] Quote from Urdal, 2004, p. 3, with information from Nazli Choucri, *Population Dynamics and International Violence: Propositions, Insights and Evidence*. Lexington, MA: Lexington, 1974, p. 73.

underemployed than men); it has an education component; and it has a duration component, among others. Consider the relationship between education levels and unemployment. There are those who argue a better education may create dissatisfaction with unemployment by creating an expectations gap between the relatively high income expected by an educated labor force and the poverty associated with high unemployment levels. As Goldstone submits, "It has typically been the case the revolutionary youth movements have been preceded by a vast expansion in secondary or higher education that exceeds the expansion in opportunities for further upward career mobility."[43] He points to a fivefold increase in the number of Iranian university students studying abroad in the two decades preceding the Shah's overthrow as supporting evidence.

Collier and others disagree, arguing instead "…there is reason to expect that a higher level of education among men rather reduces the risk of conflict, resulting from the higher opportunity cost of rebellion for educated men."[44] Collier counter-proposes that educated people have more to lose than gain from political instability, and are thus unlikely to instigate it. Thus, the role of education is not straightforward. While education increases the value of a person's labor, it may also create a frustrating expectations gap that in turns leads to political instability.

Education may also increase the duration of unemployment, because youth may require or use more time to find a job that matches their skills. And because it is arguably the "duration of unemployment, rather than its occurrence, that is most detrimental to human capital," increases in unemployment duration may cause further political instability.[45] If migration is an

---

[43] Goldstone, 1999, p. 12.
[44] Quote from Urdal, 2004, p. 4, with argument from Paul Collier, "Doing Well Out of War: An Economic Perspective," in Mats Berdal & David M. Malone, eds, *Greed & Grievance: Economic Agendas in Civil Wars.* Boulder, CO & London: Lynne Rienner, 2000, p. 91–111.
[45] Kabbani, 2005, p. 8. This is not to mention that developing states have not increased their spending on schools to keep pace with their growing youth populations. Thus, the quality of education for many of these countries has decreased. According to Graham Fuller, states across the MENA region are increasingly turning to private education that "largely falls into the hands of Islamist religious organizations, who have both the funding and the interest to assume the challenge." Fuller, 2003, p. 20.

option for these young, unemployed cohorts, it might serve as an outlet valve and defuse the potential political instability. But accurately measuring migration levels, let alone detailing the migrants' educational levels, is for all practical purposes impossible, precluding further analysis.[46] Suffice to say that migrating workers can relieve labor supply pressures in their home country, but if these migrants are highly skilled or educated, their migration represents a detrimental brain drain from the original country.[47]

Other authors have suggested unemployment is not as important as its effect, which is poverty. Still others suggest even unemployment and poverty are too generic and must be further disaggregated. According to Gurr and others, "...the mere fact that people are poor seldom produces strong grievances. Rather, violent conflicts may erupt from cases of 'relative deprivation,'" where poor, unemployed youth see themselves as deprived of something that others have.[48] They may see their relative deprivation as merely a grievance or an opportunity to obtain material resources.[49] Generational differences are not necessarily required.

Robert Kaplan also distinguished between rural and urban poverty, linking income and population density to political instability by deeming rural poverty "age old" and "almost a 'normal' part of the social fabric," but considering "urban poverty socially destabilizing." Kaplan follows by asserting, "As Iran has shown, Islamic extremism is the psychological defense mechanism of many urbanized peasants threatened with the loss of traditions in pseudo-modern cities where their values are under attack, where basic services like water and electricity are

[46] CountryWatch's 2006 Iran Country Review estimates that in 2001, "...the educated middle-class was leaving the country at a rate of 200,000 per year." CountryWatch Incorporated, 2006, p. 14. Found at: http://aol.countrywatch.com/aol_country.asp?vCOUNTRY=80.
[47] Kabbani, 2005, p. 25-26.
[48] Quote from Urdal, 2004, p. 5, with information from Ted R. Gurr, *Why Men Rebel*. Princeton, NJ: Princeton University Press, 1970.
[49] Kahl, 2002, p. 262.

unavailable, and where they are assaulted by a physically unhealthy environment."[50] To Kaplan, then, poor urban dwellers turn to Islamic extremism, which in turn leads to political instability.

A major barrier that precludes definitively linking youth unemployment to political instability is the fact that accurate data on unemployment are not necessarily available for every country every year, so youth unemployment must be estimated, interpolated, or guessed. Some analysts use per capita gross national product (GNP), per capita gross domestic product (GDP), or per capita energy consumption as proxies for unemployment, supposing these data are more available. Others submit that even these do not adequately suffice, arguing a country's involvement in international trade, in both percent level and in type of trade, is more important because "Countries with a larger portion of their gross national product (GNP) tied to international trade, and with lower infant mortality, [are] generally more stable."[51]

Besides the critique that unemployment data is not readily available, Kahl also dismisses poverty's link to political instability by arguing "The poor usually lack the requisite resources and opportunities to rebel, especially if the state is strong."[52] He, Urdal, and Homer-Dixon think the relative deprivation theory over predicts the likelihood of violence resulting from grievances. In their independent arguments, they submit grievances must be compounded by a popular movement with a collective identity (such as ethnicity, religion, class, or generation, similar to the generational consciousness rationale) as well a failed political structure or weakened state.[53]

Regime Type

The fourth and final school of thought maintains that a country's Regime Type is overwhelmingly more important than the existence of a self-conscious, motivated youth bulge.

---

[50] Kaplan, 1994, p. 66.
[51] Goldstone, 2001, p. 166; or Goldstone, 1999, p. 16.
[52] Kahl, 2002, p. 263.
[53] Kahl, 2002, p. 262; Urdal, 2005, p. 9-10; and Gleditsch and Urdal, 2002, p. 286.

Proponents of this argument often use the readily available Polity IV database to measure regime type along a continuum ranging from -10 (most autocratic) to +10 (most democratic).[54] They argue political instability is largely confined to the middle section of the spectrum, and that "The impact of regime type is generally believed to take an inverted U-shaped form, meaning that stark autocracies and fully developed democracies are both less likely to experience conflict than intermediate and unstable regimes."[55] Figure 3 below depicts graphically the relationships found in their empirical testing among youth bulges, regime types, and political instability.

Photo Removed Due to Copyright Restrictions

Fig. 3, Probability of Armed Conflict as a Function of Youth Bulges and Regime Type[56]

Their empirical testing – which found illiberal democracies were "exceptionally prone to all types of instability," with the number of instability onsets triple the number of country-years representing cases of partial democracy[57] – also meets the common sense test. Although youth might have more motivation to rebel against a starkly autocratic regime's oppressive policies or its closed recruitment processes, for example, such a starkly autocratic regime would also likely have more coercive *ability* to quell youthful uprisings before they coalesced into meaningful

[54] The Polity data maintained by Monty Marshall, Keith Jaggers, and Ted Gurr can be found at: http://www.cidcm.umd.edu/inscr/polity/.

[55] Urdal, 2004, p. 8.

[56] Ibid, p. 11.

[57] Jack A Goldstone, et. al., "A Global Forecasting Model of Political Instability." A paper prepared for presentation at the Annual Meeting of the American Political Science Association, Washington, DC, September 1-4, 2005. Found online at http://globalpolicy.gmu.edu/pitf/, p. 15.

political instability than would a weaker autocracy.[58] Starkly autocratic regimes also probably have more *will* to quell youthful uprisings, which is important because "repression that is not strong enough to suppress opponents or that is so diffuse and erratic that innocents are persecuted, or that is aimed at groups that the public considers representative and justified in their protest, can quickly undermine perceptions of the regime's effectiveness and justice."[59]

Similarly, one would expect that, in a weak democracy, youth might be empowered by their potential political impact to test the system's limits. One might also expect such a weak democracy to be unable to quell even uprisings that threaten its existence. Finally, any state widely considered illegitimate "will find it much more difficult to maintain domestic order indefinitely, regardless of its coercive power."[60]

This school of thought has its share of critiques, too. To begin with, the Regime Type hypothesis is based on the operationalized version of a youth bulge that compares the youth cohort to the total population rather than the adult population. So Urdal and others with a different definition of a youth bulge have done empirical testing that finds "economic stagnation, but not regime type, may influence the conflict propensity of youth bulges."[61] Even Jack Goldstone, one of this rationale's most prominent proponents, admits "…if the government is sufficiently inept or divided, and the population at large has sufficient grievances to turn it against the regime, a rebellion or revolution can ensue despite the absence of a youth bulge…Conversely, even a large youth cohort may either fail to adopt a revolutionary outlook, or

---

[58] Goldstone's 2001 argument is based on the Polity IV database, but he generally considers a government autocratic when it is closed to broad political participation or popular control. Goldstone, 1999, p. 10. In Urdal, 2004, p. 4, he similarly argues that "Regime characteristics may provide the incentives for youth to riot against the government, as autocratic regimes are likely to have a very closed recruitment process both for political and economic positions." See also Kahl, 2002, p. 263.
[59] Goldstone, 2001, p. 161.
[60] Kahl, 2002, p. 263.
[61] Urdal, 2004, p. 16.

to inspire a revolutionary movement across society, if a united government provides effective leadership and presides over economic success."[62]

In sum, each of these rationales adds to our understanding of the impact of a youth bulge on political stability. But no one rationale provides a compelling case to argue youth bulges cause instability. So what can then be broadly said about the relationship between youth bulges and stability? And what specific role might Iran's youth bulge play today compared to 1979? "What can be said of the presence of a youth bulge is that it makes it easier to mobilize the population for political protest; thus if other factors arise that weaken or divide the government, and create tensions among the population, then the presence of a youth bulge can be the critical factor that underpins an explosion of radicalization and intensified revolt."[63] Thus, even if a youth bulge may not cause instability in Iran or elsewhere, it is worth exploring and monitoring for its multiplier effect.

Current Problem Definition & Methodology

The U.S.-government sponsored Political Instability Task Force has identified and analyzed over 140 episodes of instability – defined as one or more instances of revolutionary war, ethnic war, adverse regime change, or genocide and politicide – from 1955-2004. Nearly 60 of those episodes occurred in Muslim nations.[64] A decade of this Task Force's work covering 117 cases of instability onset finds that "most economic, demographic, geographic, and political variables do not have consistent and statistically significant effects on the risk of instability

---

[62] Goldstone, 1999, p. 8-9.

[63] Ibid, p. 9.

[64] Data from Goldstone, 2005, and Goldstone, 2000. These Political Instability Task Force numbers do not include an adverse regime change in Iran in June 2005, though subsequent studies do. The Task Force studies noted the incidence and prevalence of instability in Muslim countries followed a sinusoidal pattern over the past 15 years: higher than it had ever previously been in the mid-1990s, declining in the late 1990s, and trending upward from 2000-2005. For the latest data, see Ted R. Gurr, et al., "Forecasting Instability: Are Ethnic Wars and Muslim Countries Different?" A paper prepared for presentation at the Annual Meeting of the American Political Science Association, Washington, DC, September 1-4, 2005. All Task Force findings and papers can be found online at http://globalpolicy.gmu.edu/pitf/.

onset."[65] Instead, the factors they find matter are "regime type, infant mortality (logged and normalized to the global mean in the year of observation), a 'bad neighborhood' indicator flagging cases with four or more bordering states embroiled in armed civil or ethnic conflict, and the presence of state-led discrimination."[66]

Given this list of significant factors, it is safe to say the Task Force falls into the "Regime Type" school of thought. Interestingly, rather than searching as Urdal has done for methods to measure a country's absorption capacity, the Political Instability Task Force's analysis suggested they instead look for independent variables that would affect a new dependent variable, state stability. After ten years of research and analysis, the Task Force believes "the origins of political crises can best be understood by turning the problem on its head, asking what factors are necessary for a state to sustain stability despite the various problems it might encounter."[67]

This Task Force further identified 48 countries where Muslims comprise at least 40% of the total population and developed a "Muslim countries model" to "identify risk factors associated with the onset of political instability" in these Muslim countries.[68] Their more specific analysis found Muslim countries were in crisis roughly one out of every four years between 1955 and 2003, in contrast to the non-Muslim world's rate of crisis being just one in seven years. Thus, "Muslim countries have experienced more political instability than non-Muslim countries for half a century."[69]

Like its parent model, the Task Force's Muslim countries model found regime type, infant mortality rate, and "bad neighborhoods" were statistically significant and played a

---

[65] Goldstone, 2005, p. 19.

[66] Ibid, p. 20.

[67] Ibid, p. 9. The results of their empirical studies are summarized in Table 1 at the back of this paper.

[68] Ted Robert Gurr, et al., "Forecasting Instability: Are Ethnic Wars and Muslim Countries Different?" A paper prepared for presentation at the Annual Meeting of the American Political Science Association, Washington, DC, September 1-4, 2005. Found online at http://globalpolicy.gmu.edu/pitf/, 2005, p. 7.

[69] Gurr, et al., 2005, p. 8-9.

powerful role in influencing the onset of political instability. But the model – whose results are summarized at Table 2 at the end of this paper – found Muslim countries "more vulnerable to instability when more bordering states are engaged in *any* type of armed conflict," not just internal conflict. The Muslim countries model therefore includes a broadened definition of what constitutes a "bad neighborhood" for Muslim countries, plus two additional significant factors:[70]

- Muslim countries ruled by ethnic or religious minorities are two to three times as likely to suffer an outbreak of instability as those under majority rule or where elite ethnicity is not politically salient; and
- The longer a chief executive's tenure, the more vulnerable a Muslim country is to an outbreak of instability, other things being equal.[71]

Before we can use these two models to compare and contrast Iran today with Iran prior to its 1979 Islamic revolution, we must first better understand the independent variables.

Regime type is clearly the most important of the variables, and though the Task Force initially used the Polity IV 21-point continuum between full autocracies and full democracies, they eventually found it less useful than a four part categorization based on the Polity IV scale's underlying components. The four parts now used by the Political Instability Task Force are:

- *Full autocracies*: regimes that combine an absence of effective contestation with repressed or suppressed participation;
- *Full democracies*: regimes that combine fully free and fair elections with open and well-institutionalized participation;
- *Partial democracies*: regimes in which top government officials are chosen through competitive elections and political participation is not effectively controlled by those officials, but that still fall short of full democracy on one or the other of those dimensions; and
- *Partial autocracies*: regimes which either hold competitive elections or allow substantial political participation outside the government's control, but not both.[72]

Consistent with other empirical work, such as Urdal's 2004 and 2005 works cited above and represented in Figure 3, the Task Force found the risk of instability lowest in full

---

[70] Ibid, p. 9.
[71] Ibid, p. 10-11.
[72] Goldstone, et al., 2005, p. 16.

democracies and full autocracies, *ceteris paribus*, and found the risk of instability highest in "hybrid" regimes – partial democracies and partial autocracies. [73]

Infant mortality rate, defined as the fraction of live-born children who die before the age of one year, is the second key independent variable to consider. It is "known to be an excellent summary measure for standard of living; it thus addresses popular perceptions of the effectiveness of the regime in providing for the popular welfare and nationalist programs of economic development."[74] The Political Instability Task Force joins Urdal and others in recognizing IMR is both strongly statistically significant and positively related to armed conflict. Further, all efforts failed at finding better proxies than IMR for a country's standard of living.[75]

Third, the Task Force included a variable to denote a country located in a "**bad neighborhood**," which it defined as four or more bordering states embroiled in armed civil or ethnic conflict. The Task Force found that, globally, the odds of instability increase dramatically when a country is surrounded by four or more neighbors with such internal conflicts. But in the Muslim countries model, recall the definition of "bad neighborhoods" was broadened to include those countries surrounded by *any* countries embroiled in *any* conflicts, internal or external.

The Political Instability Task Force's final independent variable in its global forecasting model of instability is the presence of **state-led discrimination**. The Task Force found countries

---

[73] What Goldstone, et al., found most surprising was the power of disaggregating the data even further by exploring the *level of factionalism* within the government. According to Polity, "factionalism occurs when political competition is dominated by ethnic or other parochial groups that regularly compete for political influence in order to promote particularist agendas and favor group members to the detriment of common, secular, or cross-cutting agendas." Though factionalism might be *a priori* considered only relevant to democracies, it is also "the most common form of participation in autocracies that do not repress political competition, either by design or incapacity." Its addition into the Task Force's empirical testing improved their postdictive (vice predictive) accuracy rates to at or beyond 80 percent, further validating their model and the independent variables' significance. See Goldstone, et al., 2005, p. 17.

[74] Goldstone, 2001, p. 166. See Amartya Sen's seminal work on IMR, "Mortality as an Indicator of Economic Success and Failure," in *The Economic Journal*, Vol. 108, No. 446, January 1998, p. 1-25.

[75] Goldstone, et. al., 2005, p. 10. The Task force found that "...no model, no matter how complex, performed significantly better than models that simply used infant mortality (logged and normalized) as a single indicator of standard of living."

that discriminated economically or politically against "at least one communal group track by the Minorities at Risk (MAR) project…are more than twice as likely to suffer an outbreak of instability as countries without such discrimination."[76]

Recall that the Muslim countries model added two further independent variables to improve its postdictive accuracy. The first of these is whether or not the country is ruled by an ethnic or religious minority. If it is, the country is two to three times more likely to suffer an outbreak of instability as a country under majority rule or where elite ethnicity does not matter politically. The second variable is the duration of the country's chief executive's tenure. *Ceteris paribus*, the longer a Muslim country's leader has been in power, the more vulnerable that country is to an outbreak of instability.

Iran in 1979 and 2006

At least some of the circumstances preceding Iran's 1979 Islamic Revolution appear to be similarly in place today. For example, Iran has a **youth bulge** today just as it did in 1979. According to one CIA study, "By the mid-1970s half of Iran's population was under 16 and two-thirds was under 30. This directly contributed to the street politics of 1977-79 that contributed to the fall of the Shah and the rise of a government hostile to U.S. interests."[77] Though the 1979 youth bulge ended with the deaths of thousands of soldiers during the eight-year long Iran-Iraq war, the war and its deaths sowed the seeds of today's youth bulge. Iranian leaders encouraged population growth via benefits such as allowances and food subsidies for larger families so that Iran would eventually have more youth to make soldiers.[78] Today, though Iran's total population continues to grow (see Fig. 4 at top), its youth bulge is already subsiding thanks to Tehran's

---

[76] Ibid, p. 21. The University of Maryland's Minorities at Risk (MAR) project data are available at http://www.cidcm.umd.edu/inscr/mar/.

[77] CIA, 2001.

[78] Farzaneh Roudi-Fahimi, "Iran's Family Planning Program: Responding to a Nation's Needs." Population Reference Bureau MENA Policy Brief, 2002.

successful family planning program (see Fig. 5 at bottom). According to World Bank and UN

Population Division estimates, the Iranian youth bulge should have peaked in 2005, and within

the next ten years should drop to near 15% of the populace.[79]

Photo Removed Due to Copyright Restrictions

Fig. 4, Iranian Population and Labor Force Trends[80]

Photo Removed Due to Copyright Restrictions

---

[79] United Nations Population Division (UNDP), Department of Department of Economic and Social Affairs. World Population Prospects: The 2004 Revision of the Population Database, found on-line at http://esa.un.org/unpp/; and the World Bank's Kabbani, 2005, p. 13.

[80] Source: The Conference Board and Groningen Growth and Development Centre, Total Economy Database, January 2006, found at http://www.ggdc.net.

[81] Source: UNDP Population Database.

Unfortunately, the Task Force's country-by-country analysis of **regime types** is considered classified by its U.S. government sponsor.[82] But given the category definitions above, Iran in 1979 would likely have been considered a partial autocracy. In 1979, U.S. President Jimmy Carter effectively pressured the Shah of Iran to reduce repression, thus "giving a space for opponents to undertake more active public resistance" and following the path of other regimes that were similarly "not repressive enough to crush their opponents but were repressive enough to increase perceptions of their injustice and swing elites and publics to support the opposition, strengthening the revolution."[83] Additionally, the Shah was weakened by widespread perception of ineffectiveness. He was considered "…ineffective in his inability to control inflation; as arbitrary in his attacks on bazaar merchants; and as ideologically immoral for his acceptance of Western customs and his close relationship with the United States."[84]

Today, Iran would likely be considered a full autocracy. Ayatollah Ali Khamenei, the heir to the Islamic Revolution's Ayatollah Khomeini, has ruled as Supreme Leader since 1989. Although Khamenei "lacks the unquestioned spiritual and political authority of Khomeini,…[he] appears to face no direct threats to his position."[85] Popular votes determine Iran's Presidency and election to the Majles (parliament), but the Supreme Leader maintains tight control of the twelve-member Council of Guardians and controls key appointments within the military.[86] Reform efforts in the early 2000s led by ex-President Mohammad Khatemi have largely been reversed, and the June 2005 surprise election of President Mahmoud Ahmadinejad, once the hard-line mayor of Tehran, furthered the Iranian government's swing back toward autocracy.

---

[82] Personal correspondence with Dr Jack Goldstone, 14 February 2006.
[83] Goldstone, 2001, p. 162.
[84] Goldstone, 1999, p. 11.
[85] Kenneth Katzman, "Iran: US Concerns and Policy Responses," CRS Report for Congress, Updated April 15, 2005, p. CRS-2.
[86] Ibid, p. CRS-2. Katzman notes that six Islamic jurists of the Council of Guardians' twelve members are appointed by the Supreme Leader, while the remaining six are secular lawyers are selected by the Majles.

In terms of **IMR**, the data reflected Figure 6 below show Iran's IMR has been declining steadily since the 1950s, implying continually improving standards of living for successive generations.

Photo Removed Due to Copyright Restrictions

Fig. 6, Iranian Infant Mortality Rate (per 1,000 births)[87]

But even supposing IMR was not necessarily the best measure of standard of living, and that per capita GDP was a more accurate reflection of a country's standard of living, Figure 7 below depicts graphically that, since the 1950s, Iran's total GDP and per capita GDP have both been steadily increasing. That means the absolute growth of the Iranian economy is outpacing its population growth. Further, U.S. Department of Energy estimates are that Iran's real GDP grew at about 5.6 percent in 2005 and is expected to grow by 4.8 percent in 2006, while inflation is estimated to be 15 percent annually.[88]

---

[87] Source: UNDP Population Database.
[88] United States Department of Energy (DOE) Information Administration, USG Energy Statistics found at: http://www.eia.doe.gov/emeu/cabs/Iran/Background.html.

Photo Removed Due to Copyright Restrictions

Fig. 7, Iranian GDP[89]

Third, Iran in both 1979 and 2006 could arguably be considered in the worst of "**bad**

neighborhoods." A review of the Uppsala Conflict dataset for states surrounding Iran indicates

the following:[90]

- The dataset records no conflict in the years around 1979 or 2006 for Azerbaijan or Armenia.
- Afghanistan has been at war from 1978 to the present, including regularly occurring factional fighting, the invasion and occupation by the USSR beginning in December 1979, and U.S. Global War on Terror (GWOT) operations since September 2001.
- Pakistan fought an intermediate level war against Baluchi separatists from 1975-1977. It is currently involved in the U.S. GWOT and is on a continual war-time footing against India.
- Across the Persian Gulf from Iran, the Uppsala dataset does not record any significant conflict in the years surrounding 1979 or 2006 for Oman, UAE, Qatar, or Bahrain.
- The Saudi Arabian government fought a minor war against the Juhayman movement in 1979.

---

[89] Source: The Conference Board and Groningen Growth and Development Centre, Total Economy Database, 2006.
[90] Subsequent conflict data found in Nils Petter Gleditsch, Peter Wallensteen, Mikael Eriksson, Margareta Sollenberg & Håvard Strand, 2002. "Armed Conflict 1946–2001: A New Dataset," *Journal of Peace Research* 39(5): p. 615–637. Found on-line at http://www.prio.no/cwp/ArmedConflict/.

- Iraq was involved in conflict throughout the 1970s with Kurds in the northern part of Iraq. Its initial feud with Iran in 1979 over the Shatt-al-Arab waterway spread to include disagreements over islands in the Strait of Hormuz as well as territory along their common land border, and by 1982, the stated incompatibility had widened to concern governmental power in addition to the territorial dispute. There was outright war between the countries from 1980-1988. And Iraq is fighting a determined insurgency now.

In sum, Iran was then and is now surrounded by instability, which makes it more susceptible to political instability of its own.

State-Led Discrimination

Iran has a number of ethnic, political and religious minority groups that have faced varying levels of government-led discrimination. In general, Iran's Arabs, Baluchis, Kurds and Turkmen – which primarily practice Sunni Islam – face government-sanctioned exclusionary practices and repression such as restrictions on practicing their faith, using their languages, organizing politically, and attaining political office. They have also been infrequently targeted with more violent action, such as torture and execution. For similar religious reasons, Iranian Christians have also faced "systematic, state-directed discrimination, particularly in the realm of politics" but also with respect to employment, education, public accommodations, the legal system, and property ownership.[91] Iranian Azeris, in contrast, share their Shi'a faith with the majority of Iranians, but are ethnically Azerbaijani (vice Persian) and their native language is Azeri Turkish. Azeris and Bakhtiaris, which are also Shi'a, are at little risk of explicit political, cultural, or economic discrimination as long as they are content to be part of the Iranian state.

On the other hand, as long as a Shi'a Muslim clergy that considers them heretics rules Iran, members of Iran's Baha'i religious sect will continue to be persecuted by the government and explicitly discriminated against. They are the most persecuted minority in the country,

---

[91] All information in this section is from the University of Maryland's Minorities At Risk (MAR) Project, with data on the Middle East and North Africa region found at http://www.cidcm.umd.edu/inscr/mar/assessments.asp?regionId=5.

having been mistreated for over fifty years and especially so since the 1979 Islamic Revolution. In fact, Iran's 1979 Constitution prohibits both observance of the Baha'i faith and organizations that promote its culture. Baha'i homes and personal property are sometimes confiscated or plundered by government officials; Baha'i may not seek political office or express themselves freely, and their rights during judicial proceedings and political organizing are restricted.

In the Muslim countries model, countries **ruled by ethnic or religious minorities** were found to be two to three times as likely to suffer an outbreak of instability as those under majority rule or where elite ethnicity is not politically salient. Iran is ruled today by elites who are members of an ethnic and religious majority, just as it was in 1979. The difference is that in 1979, the elites were secular and the Revolution was fomented by religious zealots who successfully capitalized on the regime's secularism to de-legitimize it.

The Muslim countries model also includes the **chief executive's tenure** as one of its independent variables. Other things being equal, the longer a Muslim country's chief executive's tenure, the more vulnerable that country is to an outbreak of instability. After Britain and the Soviet Union invaded Iran in 1941, they installed Mohammed Reza as the Shah of Iran, and he ruled until he fled the country in 1979. The Ayatollah Khameini has been the Supreme Leader since 1989, following in the Ayatollah Khomeini's footsteps.

To summarize, Iran is currently experiencing a youth bulge similar to one in 1979, when the Islamic Revolution overthrew the Shah's regime that had ruled for 38 years. Since then, Iran has experienced decreasing infant mortality rates and increasing per capita GDP; has been located in a so-called "bad neighborhood," and its government has led discrimination against different ethnic, political, and religious sects. Given these conflicting independent variables, will

Iran's autocratic regime and oil-dependent economy effectively absorb its youth bulge, or will political instability like Iran experienced in 1979 erupt once again?

			1979	**2006**
Muslim Countries Model	**Forecasting Global Instability Model**	Youth Bulge?	Yes	Yes
		Regime Type	Partial Autocracy	Full Autocracy
		IMR / Per Capita GDP	Decreasing / Increasing	Decreasing / Increasing
		Bad Neighborhood	Yes	Yes
		State-led Discrimination	Yes	Yes
		Minority Rule	No	No
		Leader's Years in Office	Shah – 38 years	Khamenei – 17 years

Today's circumstances are not likely to cause near-term political instability in Iran because strong political regimes and strong economies are the two primary variables that help states effectively absorb (if not also restrain) youth bulges. This conclusion rests on two primary logical arguments. First, if weak economies beget political instability, we should expect to see more political instability when Iran's economy struggles. Such has in fact been the case: The 1979 Islamic Revolution occurred in the midst of the late-1970s oil shocks, which helped cause Iran's GDP and per capita GDP to drop so precipitously that its economy did not begin recovering until approximately 1982. (Note the data from Figure 6 above do not reflect any significant impact of the oil shocks on Iran's steadily improving IMR.)

Today, Iran's economy is still tied to petroleum products, but its economic development measures are all improving. As long as the country can continue to sell oil to world markets its IMR, GDP, and per capita GDP are likely to continue to improve. And as long as those economic proxies are positive the likelihood of political instability in Iran is relatively low.

The logical flip side is consideration of instances of a weak economy without political instability. In Iran, weak economies have generally gone hand in hand with political instability. But before the USSR's break up, there were consistently countries throughout the communist world struggling with broken economies that effectively absorbed youth bulges and repressed political instability with hard-line autocratic regimes. Thus, a country's regime type appears to outweigh its level of economic development in determining its political stability, in line with the "Regime Type" school of thought.

Second, if weak regimes beget political instability, we should expect instability during weak regimes. Such has been the case in Iran for the last half century: when there is a strong Iranian regime there has been no significant political instability. In contrast, in 1979 the Shah's regime lacked legitimacy and effectiveness, and his weak autocracy was made weaker by demands from President Carter that Iran democratize and stop its internal repression. Revolution followed. In 2005, Iran might have been considered a partial autocracy, but its June 2005 elections and return to a conservative, hard-line stance – arguably an adverse political change in and of itself – mark a return to full autocracy for the country. We should therefore expect near-term stability.

Implications for U.S. National Security Strategy

In light of the fact that 95 percent of the earth's population growth will be in the poorest areas of the globe, the question is not whether there will be war (there will be a lot of it) but what kind of war. And who will fight whom?[92]

Robert Kaplan's prediction over a decade ago was not the first warning about the importance of demographic changes, nor will it be the last. Worldwide demographic trends such as changing age structures, urbanization, and population density movement are an increasingly important element of today's international security environment. Such trends have at least three

---

[92] Kaplan, 1994, p. 73.

kinds of security implications, according to RAND's Brian Nichiporuk: they can lead to changes in *nature of conflict*; they can affect the *nature of national power*; and they may influence the *sources of future conflict.*"[93]

Nichiporuk and others have argued that demographic changes, especially urbanization, might reduce the advantages the U.S. enjoys in long-range precision weaponry and information processing. Urban areas have significantly more line of sight impediments than would a desert or sparsely populated, sparsely built up environment, and the U.S. would have more cause to be concerned about collateral damage and potentially accidentally harming civilians.[94] For their part, Mesquida and Wiener add that "A series of analyses of demographic and war casualty data indicates that the relative prevalence of young men consistently accounts for more than one third of the variance in severity of conflicts."[95] Thus, an increasingly urbanized state with a youth bulge could present the U.S. unique challenges in the nature of conflict.

Youth bulges and other demographic shifts may also change the sources of national power, as wealthier, low population growth states see the roots of their military power "shift from manpower-intensive forces to capital-intensive forces," while high population growth states have a surplus of youth for their armed forces.[96] States with youth surfeits may subsequently be tempted to use them to threaten neighbors, even if they are at a qualitative or technological military disadvantage. Nichiporuk points to Iran's population expansion programs beginning after the 1979 Islamic Revolution, and writes that "Iran in particular threw large numbers of its youth bulge into the anti-Iraqi front, often poorly trained and serving mostly as cannon-fodder

---

[93] Nichiporuk, 2000, p. xiii. Italics added for emphasis.
[94] Ibid, p. 19-20.
[95] Mesquida and Wiener, 1999, p. 181. They measure the severity of conflicts as reported casualties.
[96] Nichiporuk, 2000, p. 27.

with high casualties."[97] Thus, youth bulges may "Increase the number of human casualties U.S. adversaries are willing to accept in battle."[98]

Finally, if youth bulges coincide with revolutions that in turn lead to armed conflict, the unstable state with a youth bulge not only has a usable pool of manpower but is also a perceived threat because it might export its revolution (explode) or collapse into chaos (implode). Either way, the state becomes a security issue for its neighboring states.[99] For example, instability in Iran could complicate things in Iraq, especially if Tehran decides to purposefully destabilize the country using its influence over Iraqi Shiite clerics, the Iraqi media, and Iraq's economy.[100]

What Can and Should the U.S. Do?

For analysts, planners and policymakers alike, the questions remain whether or not Iran's youth bulge will lead to political instability and conflict, and what can the U.S. do about it? The U.S. must first decide whether it wants stability or democracy in Iran, remembering that its decision and efforts towards its goals will have regional if not worldwide ramifications. The U.S. should therefore integrate its instruments of power toward promoting near-term stability within Iran and the surrounding region, avoiding conflict over democratization until the situations in Iraq and Afghanistan are more favorable, if possible.

On the diplomatic front, the U.S. should partner with Russia, France, Germany, and the United Kingdom to work with Iran directly – and should carefully consider working directly with Iran itself – toward peaceful long-term solutions. Part of the effort could be toward uniting Iran's youth population, workers and small business owners to take on the hard-line clerics. As

---

[97] Fuller, 2003, p. 33.
[98] CIA, 2001, p. 40.
[99] Nichiporuk, 2000, p. 29.
[100] Jay Solomon in Washington, Farnaz Fassihi in Baghdad, Iraq, and Philip Shishkin in Amarah, Iraq. "Rough Neighborhood: Iran Plays Growing Role in Iraq, Complicating Bush's Strategy; Tehran's Influence on Politics, Daily Life Could Give It Leverage in Nuclear Debate; Help for Shiite TV Stations." Wall Street Journal (Eastern Edition). New York, N.Y.: Feb 14, 2006. p. A.1.

one author points out, "Successful political movements in modern Iranian history have typically involved a coalition of social forces. Merchants of larger property, shopkeepers and artisans of the bazaar have been one key element; intellectuals and white-collar workers have been another; the Shiite clerical corps the third. Industrialization has made the working class important as well. These forces were behind the Constitutional Revolution of 1905-11, the Mossadegh oil nationalization movement of 1951-1953 and the Islamic Revolution of 1978-79."[101]

The U.S. should also temper its plans to overtly spur democracy and freedom in Iran outlined by Secretary of State Condoleezza Rice to a congressional budget hearing in February. According to Rice, President Bush is requesting $75 million in his supplemental budget request for 2006 to confront the "aggressive policies of the Iranian regime" by broadcasting U.S. radio and television programs into Iran and by paying for Iranians to study in America.[102]

If the U.S. wants to support freedoms it must also be willing to accept the consequences of its support, including the possibility of a democratized Iran that is not pro-U.S.[103] It must keep in mind that efforts to move Iran away from autocracy may also move the country away from the stability enforced by the autocratic regime. As Goldstone, et al., remark, "It is perhaps ironic that policies aimed at spreading democracy tend to focus on the first two elements—ensuring open and competitive elections and limiting executive authority—when our research suggests that *it is how these elements are combined with the character of political participation that substantially determines how resistant regimes are to political instability.*"[104]

---

[101] Juan Cole, "Aiding Iran's Students," *The Nation*, 14 July 2003, p. 6.
[102] See also Fuller, 2003, p. 39-40. Fuller suggests the U.S. ought to do significantly more to further Iran's understanding of U.S. ideals – freedom, liberty, non-discrimination, rule of law, human rights, civil liberties, justice, equality, and equal opportunity.
[103] This scenario is close to what happened with recent Palestinian Authority elections, when Hamas wrested power from the Fatah party.
[104] Goldstone, et. al., 2005, p. 18. Italics in the original.

Part of the U.S. answer should clearly be informational. The U.S. needs to work more diligently to ensure Iranians and the world at large understand the U.S. has no hegemonic intent toward Iran. The U.S. also needs to improve efforts toward demonstrating Iran's ruling theocracy is not just repressing the Iranian people and economy but also poses a threat to regional security. Though Iran's theocracy clings to its religion as a shield, the U.S. may be able to effectively use that religion as a weapon against the regime by pointing out regime failures. As Graham Fuller has pointed out, "Islamism serves as a vehicle of protest everywhere *except where it is in power*, such as in Iran and Sudan. It is the *status quo* that is the major target of anger."[105] If the youth bulge is going to be rebellious over the status quo, the U.S. must find ways to mobilize and channel that youthful energy to affect change toward its ends.[106]

Militarily, the U.S. should closely monitor Iranian indications and warnings signatures, especially its "…trends in age structure, urban slum growth, rural landlessness, ethnic growth rate imbalances, and other demographic factors."[107] Intelligence analysts and military planners ought to consider demographic factors such as trends in the size, shape and duration of youth bulges, the specifics of regime type, and levels of economic development (IMR and GDP/per capita GDP).[108] Iran's long-term demographic trends – specifically its youth bulge and its growing population – make significant increases in military spending unlikely, so Iran is not likely to revolutionize its military capabilities in the near future.[109] But its demographic changes

---

[105] Fuller, 2003, p. 31. Italics in the original.

[106] Ibid, p. 25.

[107] Richard P. Cincotta, "Demographic Security Comes of Age," *ECSP Report*, Issue 10, 2004, 2004, p. 4.

[108] Goldstone (1999, p. 22) argues they should also scrutinize rates of educational expansion compared to economic expansion, and be especially wary of states with a wide disparity between the rate of annual secondary/tertiary graduates and the rate of economic expansion.

[109] According to Hughes' 1997 testimony, "Iran's primary long-range goal is to establish itself as the pan-Islamic leader throughout the Middle East region and beyond. In pursuit of that goal it requires military forces that can deter or defeat Iraq, intimidate its Gulf Arab neighbors, and limit the regional influence of the West – particularly the United States." Iran must improve its military to do that, but cannot expect more than "slow but steady" military

may affect Iran's internal stability, which in turn affects neighboring countries. Thus, when demographic trends indicate increased likelihood of political instability, U.S. military planners should ensure flexible deterrent options are properly tailored to the situation and that military operations plans are current.

Economically, the U.S. should use both carrot and stick approaches toward Iran. It could offer direct economic incentives or push initiatives in the UN or other international bodies that target aid precisely to stop the causes and manage the effects of rapid population growth, including funding programs that reduce fertility rates and increase education levels, especially for women.[110] The U.S. could also pursue multi-lateral or international sanctions against sales of Iranian oil and petroleum products. In fact, the Iranian government actually *expects* the U.S. to follow such a path.[111] But if economic shock is one of the things required for social and political upheaval, U.S. sanctions on Iran may not only be ineffective, they may also be counter-productive. The Bush Administration must seriously consider whether it wants *stability* or *democracy* in Iran, because they are not the same thing. And as Hamas and the Palestinian Authority election should have recently taught, the U.S. needs to be careful what it asks for because it may just get it.

Conclusion

Demographics have become an increasingly important part of the international security arena, representing challenges, vulnerabilities, options and opportunities for countries facing them. Though some demographers argue the certainty of demographics, "The demographic

---

progress for the foreseeable future. Thus, Iran will almost certainly continue to suffer with its current force shortcomings until its youth bulge passes.

[110] Nichiporuk, 2000, p. xx.

[111] In a televised speech following Tehran's 14 Feb 2006 announcement it would resume its uranium enrichment efforts in defiance of international pressure to stop its nuclear program, Iranian President Mahmoud Amahdinejad warned Iranians to expect economic sanctions in the coming months. Molly Moore, "Iran Restarts Uranium Program; Enhanced Access For U.N. Inspectors Halted at Facilities." *Washington Post*, 15 February 2006, p. A01.

future is anything but certain; demographic trends are not immutable."[112] Some governments, including Iran, may be able to pursue policies and agendas that take advantage of them, hopefully achieving positive demographic dividends. Other governments will fail to cope and will fall because of them. As long as Iran continues to subsidize its economy by selling oil/petroleum products and as long as its autocratic regime maintains its tight-fisted control, its youth bulge should move into a "middle age" bulge that is historically more stable.

But Iran's situation is precarious, nevertheless. It may have an autocratic regime and an improving level of economic development, but it is also pursuing a uranium enrichment agenda that may turn international opinion against it, causing change in one or both of these areas. U.S. and international efforts must carefully balance their change agendas with the possibility of causing unintended side effects leading to political instability. The greater danger is that political instability in Iran may spill over to other countries in a region suffering from some of the same demographic trends as Iran but without the regime or economic strength to effectively cope with them.

---

[112] Cincotta, 2004, p. 4.

BIBLIOGRAPHY

Abbasi-Shavazi, Mohammad Jalal. "Below replacement-level fertility in Iran: Progress and Prospects." A paper prepared for the IUSSP Seminar on: International Perspectives on Low Fertility: Trends, Theories and Policies, Tokyo, March 21-23, 2001.

Barnett, Thomas P. M. *The Pentagon's New Map: War and Peace in the Twenty-First Century.* G.P. Putnam's Sons, New York, 2004.

Central Intelligence Agency (CIA). *Long-Term Demographic Trends*, 2001. Found at http://www.cia.gov/cia/reports/Demo_Trends_For_Web.pdf.

Choucri, Nazli. *Population Dynamics and International Violence: Propositions, Insights and Evidence.* Lexington, MA: Lexington, 1974.

Cincotta, Richard P. "Demographic Security Comes of Age," *ECSP Report*, Issue 10, 2004.

Cole, Juan. "Aiding Iran's Students," *The Nation*, 14 July 2003, p. 6

Collier, Paul. "Doing Well Out of War: An Economic Perspective," in Mats Berdal & David M. Malone, eds, *Greed & Grievance: Economic Agendas in Civil Wars.* Boulder, CO & London: Lynne Rienner, 2000, p. 91–111.

Conference Board and Groningen Growth and Development Centre. Total Economy Database, January 2006, found at http://www.ggdc.net.

Cordesman, Anthony H. "The U.S. Military and the Evolving Challenges in the Middle East." *Naval War College Review*, Vol. 55, No. 3, Summer 2002, p. 72-112.

CountryWatch Incorporated. Iran Country Watch, 2006. Found at: http://aol.countrywatch.com/aol_country.asp?vCOUNTRY=80.

Eisenstadt, S.N. *From Generation to Generation: Age Groups and Social Structure.* New York: Free Press, 1971.

Fair, C. Christine. "Iran: What Future for the Islamic State?" Chapter Four in *The Muslim World after 9/11*, a RAND Corporation Project Air Force study, 2004, p. 207-245.

Fuller, Graham E. "The Youth Factor: The New Demographics of the Middle East and the Implications for U.S. Policy." DRAFT, 18 January 2003.

Gleditsch, Nils Petter, and Henrik Urdal. "Ecoviolence? Links Between Population Growth, Environmental Scarcity and Violent Conflict in Thomas Homer-Dixon's Work." *Journal of International Affairs*, Fall 2002, vol., 56., no. 1., p. 283-301.

Gleditsch, Nils Petter, Peter Wallensteen, Mikael Eriksson, Margareta Sollenberg & Håvard Strand, 2002. "Armed Conflict 1946–2001: A New Dataset," *Journal of Peace Research* 39(5): p. 615–637. Found on-line at http://www.prio.no/cwp/ArmedConflict/.

Goldstone, Jack A., et. al. "A Global Forecasting Model of Political Instability." A paper prepared for presentation at the Annual Meeting of the American Political Science Association, Washington, DC, September 1-4, 2005. Found online at http://globalpolicy.gmu.edu/pitf/.

Goldstone, Jack A. "Population And Security: How Demographic Change Can Lead To Violent Conflict." *Journal of International Affairs*, Fall 2002, vol. 56, no. 1, p. 13–21.

Goldstone, Jack A. "Toward A Fourth Generation Of Revolutionary Theory." *Annual Review of Political Science*, 2001, 4: p. 139–187.

Goldstone, Jack A. "Youth Bulges, Youth Cohorts, and their Contribution to Periods of Rebellion and Revolution," unpublished manuscript prepared for the John M. Olin Center for Strategic Studies, Harvard University, Center for International Affairs, 29 May 1999.

Goldstone, Jack A., Ted Robert Gurr, Barbara Harff, Marc A. Levy, Monty G. Marshall, Robert H. Bates, David L. Epstein, Colin H. Kahl, Pamela T. Surko, John Ulfelder, and Alan N. Unger. 2000. *State Failure Task Force Report: Phase III Findings*. McLean, VA: Science Applications International Corporation (SAIC).

Gurr, Ted R., et al., "Forecasting Instability: Are Ethnic Wars and Muslim Countries Different?" A paper prepared for presentation at the Annual Meeting of the American Political Science Association, Washington, DC, September 1-4, 2005. Found online at http://globalpolicy.gmu.edu/pitf/.

Gurr, Ted R. *Why Men Rebel*. Princeton, NJ: Princeton University Press, 1970.

Helgerson, John. L. "The National Security Implications of Global Demographic Change." Address to the Denver World Affairs Council and the Better World Campaign, Denver, CO, 30 April 2002. Found at http://www.au.af.mil/au/awc/awcgate/cia/helgerson2.htm.

Hendrixson, Anne. "The 'Youth Bulge': Defining the Next Generation of Young Men as a Threat to the Future." *Population & Development Program*, Hampshire College, No. 19, Winter 2003.

Hughes, Patrick M., Lieutenant General, USA. "Global Threats and Challenges to the United States and Its Interests Abroad," Statement for the Senate Select Committee on Intelligence, 5 Feb 1997 and Statement for the Senate Armed Services Committee on Intelligence, 6 Feb 1997. Found at http://www.fas.org/irp/congress/1997_hr/s970205.htm.

Huntington, Samuel. *The Clash Of Civilizations And The Remaking Of World Order*. New York: Simon & Schuster, 1996.

Kabbani, Nader, and Ekta Kothari. *Youth Employment in the MENA Region: A Situational Assessment*. The World Bank. Social Protection Discussion Paper No. 0534, September 2005.

Kahl, Colin. "Demographic Change, Natural Resources and Violence: The Current Debate." *Journal of International Affairs*, Fall 2002, vol. 56, no. 1, p. 257-282.

Kaplan, Robert. "The Coming Anarchy," *Atlantic Monthly*, February, 1994, p. 44-76.

Katzman, Kenneth. "Iran: US Concerns and Policy Responses," CRS Report for Congress, Updated April 15, 2005.

Kent, Mary M., and Carl Haub. "Global Demographic Divide," *Population Bulletin*, Population Reference Bureau, Vol. 60, No. 4, December 2005.

Laipson, Ellen. "The Middle East's Demographic Transition: What Does it Mean?" *Journal of International Affairs*, Fall 2002, vol. 56, no. 1, p. 175-188.

Mannheim, Karl. "What is a Social Generation?" In *The Youth Revolution: The Conflict of Generations in Modern History*, edited by Anthony Esler, p. 7-14. Lexington, MA: D.C. Heath, 1974.

Mannheim, Karl. *From Karl Mannheim*. Edited by Kurt Wolff. 2nd ed. New Brunswick, NJ: Transaction Publishers, 1993.

McAdam, Doug. *Freedom Summer*. Oxford: Oxford University Press, 1988.

Mesquida, Christian G., and Neil I. Wiener. "Male Age Composition and Severity of Conflicts." *Politics and the Life Sciences*, September 1999, 18, p. 181–189.

Moller, Herbert. "Youth as a Force in the Modern World," *Comparative Studies in Society and History*, Vol. 10, No. 3 (April, 1968), p. 237-260.

Moore, Molly. "Iran Restarts Uranium Program; Enhanced Access For U.N. Inspectors Halted at Facilities." *Washington Post*, 15 February 2006, p. A01.

Nichiporuk, Brian. "Regional Demographics and the War on Terrorism." Royal United Services Institute for Defence Studies, United Kingdom. *RUSI Journal*, Vol. 148, No. 1, February 2003, p. 22-29.

Nichiporuk, Brian. *The Security Dynamics of Demographic Factors*. RAND Monograph Report, Document Number MR-1088-WFHF/RF/DLPF/A, Santa Monica, 2000.

Population Reference Bureau. *2005 World Population Data Sheet*. Found at
http://www.prb.org/.

Roudi-Fahimi, Farzaneh. "Iran's Family Planning Program: Responding to a Nation's Needs."
Population Reference Bureau, MENA Policy Brief, 2002.

Sciolino, Elaine. "Radicalism: Is the Devil in the Demographics?" New York Times, 9
December 2001.

Sen, Amartya. "Mortality as an Indicator of Economic Success and Failure." *The Economic
Journal*, Vol. 108, No. 446, January 1998, p. 1-25.

Solomon, Jay in Washington, Farnaz Fassihi in Baghdad, Iraq, and Philip Shishkin in Amarah,
Iraq. "Rough Neighborhood: Iran Plays Growing Role in Iraq, Complicating Bush's
Strategy; Tehran's Influence on Politics, Daily Life Could Give It Leverage in Nuclear
Debate; Help for Shiite TV Stations." Wall Street Journal (Eastern Edition). New York,
N.Y. Feb 14, 2006. p. A.1.

United Nations Population Division, Department of Department of Economic and Social Affairs.
World Population Prospects: The 2004 Revision of the Population Database, found on-
line at http://esa.un.org/unpp/.

United Nations Population Division. "The Diversity of Changing Population Age Structures in
the World." United Nations Expert Group Meeting on Social and Economic Implications
of Changing Age Structure. Population Division, Department of Economic and Social
Affairs, United Nations Secretariat. Mexico City, 31 August – 2 September, 2005.
(Published 25 Aug 2005).

United States Census Bureau. International Database, found at
http://www.census.gov/ipc/www/idbnew.html.

United States Department of Energy (DOE) Information Administration. USG Energy Statistics
found at: http://www.eia.doe.gov/emeu/cabs/Iran/Background.html.

University of Maryland. Minorities At Risk (MAR) Project, with data on the Middle East and
North Africa region found at:
http://www.cidcm.umd.edu/inscr/mar/assessments.asp?regionId=5.

Urdal, Henrik. "The Devil in the Demographics: The Effect of Youth Bulges on Domestic
Armed Conflict, 1950-2000." The World Bank, Social Development Papers, Conflict
Prevention & Reconstruction, Paper No. 14, July 2004.

Urdal, Henrik. "A Clash of Generations? Youth Bulges and Political Violence." Centre for the
Study of Civil War, International Peace Research Institute, Oslo. Paper prepared for the
Workshop on Conflict Research, January 2005.

Waterbury, John. "Hate Your Policies, Love Your Institutions." *Foreign Affairs*, Jan/Feb 2003.
Vol. 82, Iss. 1, p. 58.

Zakaria, Fareed. "The Politics of Rage: Why Do They Hate Us?" *Newsweek*, 15 October 2001,
p. 22.